The Key Facts™ on the United Kingdom

Essential Information on the United Kingdom

By Patrick W. Nee

The Internationalist®
www.internationalist.com

The Internationalist®

International Business, Investment, and Travel

Published by:

The Internationalist Publishing Company

96 Walter Street/ Suite 200

Boston, MA 02131, USA

Tel: 617-354-7722

www.internationalist.com

PN@internationalist.com

Copyright © 2013 by PWN

The Internationalist is a Registered Trademark. "Key Facts" and "The Internationalist Business Guides" are Trademarks of The Internationalist Publishing Company.

All Rights are reserved under International, Pan-American, and Pan-Asian Conventions. No part of this book may be reproduced in any form without the written permission of the publisher. All rights vigorously enforced

Table Of Contents

Chapter 1: Introduction

Chapter 2: Geography

Chapter 3: People and Society

Chapter 4: Government and Key Leaders

Chapter 5: Economy

Chapter 6: Energy

Chapter 7: Communications

Chapter 8: Transportation

Chapter 9: Military

Chapter 10: Transnational Issues

Map of the United Kingdom

Chapter 1: Introduction

Background:

The United Kingdom has historically played a leading role in developing parliamentary democracy and in advancing literature and science. At its zenith in the 19th century, the British Empire stretched over one-fourth of the earth's surface. The first half of the 20th century saw the UK's strength seriously depleted in two world wars and the Irish Republic's withdrawal from the union. The second half witnessed the dismantling of the Empire and the UK rebuilding itself into a modern and prosperous European nation. As one of five permanent members of the UN Security Council and a founding member of NATO and the Commonwealth, the UK pursues a global approach to foreign policy. The UK is also an active member of the EU, although it chose to remain outside the Economic and Monetary Union. The Scottish Parliament, the National Assembly for Wales, and the Northern Ireland Assembly were established in 1999. The latter was suspended until May 2007 due to wrangling over the peace process, but devolution was fully completed in March 2010.

Chapter 2: Geography

Location:
   Western Europe, islands - including the northern one-sixth of the island of Ireland - between the North Atlantic Ocean and the North Sea; northwest of France

Geographic coordinates:
   54 00 N, 2 00 W

Map references:
   Europe

Area:
   total: 243,610 sq km
   country comparison to the world: 80
   land: 241,930 sq km
   water: 1,680 sq km
   note: includes Rockall and Shetland Islands

Area - comparative:
   slightly smaller than Oregon

Land boundaries:
   total: 360 km
   border countries: Ireland 360 km

Coastline:
   12,429 km

Maritime claims:
    territorial sea: 12 nm
    exclusive fishing zone: 200 nm
    continental shelf: as defined in continental shelf orders or in accordance with agreed upon boundaries

Climate:
    temperate; moderated by prevailing southwest winds over the North Atlantic Current; more than one-half of the days are overcast

Terrain:
    mostly rugged hills and low mountains; level to rolling plains in east and southeast

Elevation extremes:
    lowest point: The Fens -4 m
    highest point: Ben Nevis 1,343 m

Natural resources:
    coal, petroleum, natural gas, iron ore, lead, zinc, gold, tin, limestone, salt, clay, chalk, gypsum, potash, silica sand, slate, arable land

Land use:
    arable land: 24.88%
    permanent crops: 0.18%
    other: 74.93% (2011)

Irrigated land:

2,280 sq km (2005)

Total renewable water resources:

147 cu km (2011)

Freshwater withdrawal (domestic/industrial/agricultural):

total: 13.03 cu km/yr (58%/33%/9%)

per capita: 213.2 cu m/yr (2008)

Natural hazards:

winter windstorms; floods

Environment - current issues:

continues to reduce greenhouse gas emissions (has met Kyoto Protocol target of a 12.5% reduction from 1990 levels and intends to meet the legally binding target and move toward a domestic goal of a 20% cut in emissions by 2010); by 2005 the government reduced the amount of industrial and commercial waste disposed of in landfill sites to 85% of 1998 levels and recycled or composted at least 25% of household waste, increasing to 33% by 2015

Environment - international agreements:

party to: Air Pollution, Air Pollution-Nitrogen Oxides, Air Pollution-Persistent Organic Pollutants, Air Pollution-Sulfur 94, Air Pollution-Volatile Organic Compounds, Antarctic-Environmental

Protocol, Antarctic-Marine Living Resources, Antarctic Seals, Antarctic Treaty, Biodiversity, Climate Change, Climate Change-Kyoto Protocol, Desertification, Endangered Species, Environmental Modification, Hazardous Wastes, Law of the Sea, Marine Dumping, Marine Life Conservation, Ozone Layer Protection, Ship Pollution, Tropical Timber 83, Tropical Timber 94, Wetlands, Whaling
<u>signed, but not ratified</u>: none of the selected agreements

Geography - note:

lies near vital North Atlantic sea lanes; only 35 km from France and linked by tunnel under the English Channel; because of heavily indented coastline, no location is more than 125 km from tidal waters

Chapter 3: People and Society

Nationality:
>noun: Briton(s), British (collective plural)
>
>adjective: British

Ethnic groups:
>white (of which English 83.6%, Scottish 8.6%, Welsh 4.9%, Northern Irish 2.9%) 92.1%, black 2%, Indian 1.8%, Pakistani 1.3%, mixed 1.2%, other 1.6% (2001 census)

Languages:
>English
>
>note: the following are recognized regional languages: Scots (about 30% of the population of Scotland), Scottish Gaelic (about 60,000 in Scotland), Welsh (about 20% of the population of Wales), Irish (about 10% of the population of Northern Ireland), Cornish (some 2,000 to 3,000 in Cornwall)

Religions:
>Christian (Anglican, Roman Catholic, Presbyterian, Methodist) 71.6%, Muslim 2.7%, Hindu 1%, other 1.6%, unspecified or none 23.1% (2001 census)

Population:
>63,395,574 (July 2013 est.)

country comparison to the world: 22

Age structure:

0-14 years: 17.3% (male 5,625,040/female 5,346,815)

15-24 years: 12.8% (male 4,158,813/female 3,986,831)

25-54 years: 41.1% (male 13,250,434/female 12,807,328)

55-64 years: 11.5% (male 3,589,345/female 3,680,392)

65 years and over: 17.3% (male 4,877,079/female 6,073,497) (2013 est.)

Median age:

total: 40.2 years

male: 39 years

female: 41.2 years (2012 est.)

Population growth rate:

0.553% (2012 est.)

country comparison to the world: 146

Birth rate:

12.27 births/1,000 population (2012 est.)

country comparison to the world: 162

Death rate:

9.33 deaths/1,000 population (July 2012 est.)

country comparison to the world: 60

Net migration rate:

   2.59 migrant(s)/1,000 population (2012 est.)

   country comparison to the world: 29

Urbanization:

   urban population: 80% of total population (2010)

   rate of urbanization: 0.7% annual rate of change (2010-15 est.)

Major cities - population:

   LONDON (capital) 8.615 million; Birmingham 2.296 million; Manchester 2.247 million; West Yorkshire 1.541 million; Glasgow 1.166 million (2009)

Sex ratio:

   at birth: 1.05 male(s)/female

   under 15 years: 1.05 male(s)/female

   15-64 years: 1.02 male(s)/female

   65 years and over: 0.8 male(s)/female

   total population: 0.99 male(s)/female (2011 est.)

Maternal mortality rate:

   12 deaths/100,000 live births (2010)

   country comparison to the world: 146

Infant mortality rate:

   total: 4.56 deaths/1,000 live births

   country comparison to the world: 188

   male: 5 deaths/1,000 live births

female: 4.1 deaths/1,000 live births (2012 est.)

Life expectancy at birth:

total population: 80.17 years

country comparison to the world: 30

male: 78.05 years

female: 82.4 years (2012 est.)

Total fertility rate:

1.9 children born/woman (2013 est.)

country comparison to the world: 140

Health expenditures:

9.6% of GDP (2010)

country comparison to the world: 32

Physicians density:

2.739 physicians/1,000 population (2009)

Hospital bed density:

3.3 beds/1,000 population (2009)

Sanitation facility access:

improved:

urban: 100% of population

rural: 100% of population

total: 100% of population (2010 est.)

HIV/AIDS - adult prevalence rate:

0.2% (2009 est.)

country comparison to the world: 104

HIV/AIDS - people living with HIV/AIDS:
> 85,000 (2009 est.)
>
> country comparison to the world: 44

HIV/AIDS - deaths:
> fewer than 1,000 (2009 est.)
>
> country comparison to the world: 68

Obesity - adult prevalence rate:
> 22.7% (2002)
>
> country comparison to the world: 16

Education expenditures:
> 5.6% of GDP (2009)
>
> country comparison to the world: 52

Literacy:
> definition: age 15 and over has completed five or more years of schooling
>
> total population: 99%
>
> male: 99%
>
> female: 99% (2003 est.)

School life expectancy (primary to tertiary education):
> total: 16 years
>
> male: 16 years
>
> female: 17 years (2008)

Unemployment, youth ages 15-24:
> total: 19.1%

country comparison to the world: 64
male: 21.2%
female: 16.8% (2010)

Chapter 4: Government and Key Leaders

Country name:
>   conventional long form: United Kingdom of Great Britain and Northern Ireland; note - Great Britain includes England, Scotland, and Wales
>   conventional short form: United Kingdom
>   abbreviation: UK

Government type:
>   constitutional monarchy and Commonwealth realm

Capital:
>   name: London
>   geographic coordinates: 51 30 N, 0 05 W
>   time difference: UTC 0 (5 hours ahead of Washington, DC during Standard Time)
>   daylight saving time: +1hr, begins last Sunday in March; ends last Sunday in October
>   note: applies to the United Kingdom proper, not to its overseas dependencies or territories

Administrative divisions:
>   England: 27 two-tier counties, 32 London boroughs and 1 City of London or Greater London, 36 metropolitan districts, 56 unitary authorities (including 4 single-tier counties*)

<u>two-tier counties</u>: Buckinghamshire, Cambridgeshire, Cumbria, Derbyshire, Devon, Dorset, East Sussex, Essex, Gloucestershire, Hampshire, Hertfordshire, Kent, Lancashire, Leicestershire, Lincolnshire, Norfolk, North Yorkshire, Northamptonshire, Nottinghamshire, Oxfordshire, Somerset, Staffordshire, Suffolk, Surrey, Warwickshire, West Sussex, Worcestershire

<u>London boroughs and City of London or Greater London</u>: Barking and Dagenham, Barnet, Bexley, Brent, Bromley, Camden, Croydon, Ealing, Enfield, Greenwich, Hackney, Hammersmith and Fulham, Haringey, Harrow, Havering, Hillingdon, Hounslow, Islington, Kensington and Chelsea, Kingston upon Thames, Lambeth, Lewisham, City of London, Merton, Newham, Redbridge, Richmond upon Thames, Southwark, Sutton, Tower Hamlets, Waltham Forest, Wandsworth, Westminster

<u>metropolitan districts</u>: Barnsley, Birmingham, Bolton, Bradford, Bury, Calderdale, Coventry, Doncaster, Dudley, Gateshead, Kirklees, Knowlsey, Leeds, Liverpool, Manchester, Newcastle upon Tyne, North Tyneside, Oldham, Rochdale, Rotherham, Salford, Sandwell, Sefton, Sheffield, Solihull, South Tyneside,

St. Helens, Stockport, Sunderland, Tameside, Trafford, Wakefield, Walsall, Wigan, Wirral, Wolverhampton

unitary authorities: Bath and North East Somerset, Blackburn with Darwen, Bedford, Blackpool, Bournemouth, Bracknell Forest, Brighton and Hove, City of Bristol, Central Bedfordshire, Cheshire East, Cheshire West and Chester, Cornwall, Darlington, Derby, Durham County*, East Riding of Yorkshire, Halton, Hartlepool, Herefordshire*, Isle of Wight*, Isles of Scilly, City of Kingston upon Hull, Leicester, Luton, Medway, Middlesbrough, Milton Keynes, North East Lincolnshire, North Lincolnshire, North Somerset, Northumberland*, Nottingham, Peterborough, Plymouth, Poole, Portsmouth, Reading, Redcar and Cleveland, Rutland, Shropshire, Slough, South Gloucestershire, Southampton, Southend-on-Sea, Stockton-on-Tees, Stoke-on-Trent, Swindon, Telford and Wrekin, Thurrock, Torbay, Warrington, West Berkshire, Wiltshire, Windsor and Maidenhead, Wokingham, York

Northern Ireland: 26 district council areas

district council areas: Antrim, Ards, Armagh, Ballymena, Ballymoney, Banbridge, Belfast,

Carrickfergus, Castlereagh, Coleraine, Cookstown, Craigavon, Derry, Down, Dungannon, Fermanagh, Larne, Limavady, Lisburn, Magherafelt, Moyle, Newry and Mourne, Newtownabbey, North Down, Omagh, Strabane

<u>Scotland</u>: 32 council areas

<u>council areas</u>: Aberdeen City, Aberdeenshire, Angus, Argyll and Bute, Clackmannanshire, Dumfries and Galloway, Dundee City, East Ayrshire, East Dunbartonshire, East Lothian, East Renfrewshire, City of Edinburgh, Eilean Siar (Western Isles), Falkirk, Fife, Glasgow City, Highland, Inverclyde, Midlothian, Moray, North Ayrshire, North Lanarkshire, Orkney Islands, Perth and Kinross, Renfrewshire, Shetland Islands, South Ayrshire, South Lanarkshire, Stirling, The Scottish Borders, West Dunbartonshire, West Lothian

<u>Wales</u>: 22 unitary authorities

<u>unitary authorities</u>: Blaenau Gwent; Bridgend; Caerphilly; Cardiff; Carmarthenshire; Ceredigion; Conwy; Denbighshire; Flintshire; Gwynedd; Isle of Anglesey; Merthyr Tydfil; Monmouthshire; Neath Port Talbot; Newport; Pembrokeshire; Powys;

Rhondda Cynon Taff; Swansea; The Vale of Glamorgan; Torfaen; Wrexham

Dependent areas:

Anguilla, Bermuda, British Indian Ocean Territory, British Virgin Islands, Cayman Islands, Falkland Islands, Gibraltar, Montserrat, Pitcairn Islands, Saint Helena, Ascension, and Tristan da Cunha, South Georgia and the South Sandwich Islands, Turks and Caicos Islands

Independence:

12 April 1927 (Royal and Parliamentary Titles Act establishes current name of the United Kingdom of Great Britain and Northern Ireland); notable earlier dates: 927 (minor English kingdoms united); 3 March 1284 (enactment of the Statute of Rhuddlan uniting England and Wales); 1536 (Act of Union formally incorporates England and Wales); 1 May 1707 (Acts of Union formally unite England and Scotland as Great Britain); 1 January 1801 (Acts of Union formally unite Great Britain and Ireland as the United Kingdom of Great Britain and Ireland); 6 December 1921 (Anglo-Irish Treaty formalizes partition of Ireland; six counties remain part of the United Kingdom and Northern Ireland)

National holiday:
>the UK does not celebrate one particular national holiday

Constitution:
>unwritten; partly statutes, partly common law and practice

Legal system:
>common law system; has nonbinding judicial review of Acts of Parliament under the Human Rights Act of 1998

International law organization participation:
>accepts compulsory ICJ jurisdiction with reservations; accepts ICCt jurisdiction

Suffrage:
>18 years of age; universal

Executive branch:
><u>chief of state</u>: Queen ELIZABETH II (since 6 February 1952); Heir Apparent Prince CHARLES (son of the queen, born 14 November 1948)
>
><u>head of government</u>: Prime Minister David CAMERON (since 11 May 2010)
>
><u>cabinet</u>: Cabinet of Ministers appointed by the prime minister

elections: the monarchy is hereditary; following legislative elections, the leader of the majority party or the leader of the majority coalition usually becomes the prime minister

Legislative branch:
bicameral Parliament consists of House of Lords; note - membership is not fixed (788 seats; consisting of approximately 670 life peers, 92 hereditary peers, and 26 clergy - as of 1 April 2012) and House of Commons (650 seats since 2010 elections; members elected by popular vote to serve five-year terms unless the House is dissolved earlier)

elections: House of Lords - no elections (note - in 1999, as provided by the House of Lords Act, elections were held in the House of Lords to determine the 92 hereditary peers who would remain there; elections are held only as vacancies in the hereditary peerage arise); House of Commons - last held on 6 May 2010 (next to be held by June 2015)

election results: House of Commons - percent of vote by party - Conservative 36.1%, Labor 29%, Liberal Democrats 23%, other 11.9%; seats by party - Conservative 305, Labor 258, Liberal Democrat 57, other 30 note: in 1998 elections were held for a Northern Ireland Assembly (because of unresolved disputes among existing parties, the transfer of power from London to Northern Ireland came only at the end of 1999 and has been suspended four times, the latest occurring in October 2002 and lasting until 8 May 2007); in 1999, the UK held the first elections for a Scottish Parliament and a Welsh Assembly; the most recent elections for the Northern Ireland Assembly, the Scottish Parliament, and the Welsh Assembly took place in May 2011

Judicial branch:

Supreme Court of the UK (established in October 2009 taking over appellate jurisdiction formerly vested in the House of Lords is the final court of appeal); Senior Courts of England and Wales (comprising the Court of Appeal, the High Court of Justice, and the Crown Courts); Court of Judicature (Northern Ireland); Scotland's Court of Session and High Court of the Justiciary

Political parties and leaders:

Conservative [David CAMERON]; Democratic Unionist Party or DUP (Northern Ireland) [Peter ROBINSON]; Labor Party [Ed MILIBAND]; Liberal

Democrats (Lib Dems) [Nick CLEGG]; Party of Wales (Plaid Cymru) [Leanne WOOD]; Scottish National Party or SNP [Alex SALMOND]; Sinn Fein (Northern Ireland) [Gerry ADAMS]; Social Democratic and Labor Party or SDLP (Northern Ireland) [Alasdair MCDONNELL]; Ulster Unionist Party (Northern Ireland) [Mike NESBITT]; United Kingdom Independent Party or UKIP [Nigel FARAGE]

Political pressure groups and leaders:

Campaign for Nuclear Disarmament; Confederation of British Industry; National Farmers' Union; Trades Union Congress

International organization participation:

ADB (nonregional member), AfDB (nonregional member), Arctic Council (observer), Australia Group, BIS, C, CBSS (observer), CD, CDB, CE, CERN, EAPC, EBRD, EIB, EITI (implementing country), ESA, EU, FAO, FATF, G-20, G-5, G-7, G-8, G-10, IADB, IAEA, IBRD, ICAO, ICC (national committees), ICRM, IDA, IEA, IFAD, IFC, IFRCS, IGAD (partners), IHO, ILO, IMF, IMO, IMSO, Interpol, IOC, IOM, IPU, ISO, ITSO, ITU, ITUC (NGOs), MIGA, MONUSCO, NATO, NEA, NSG,

OAS (observer), OECD, OPCW, OSCE, Paris Club, PCA, PIF (partner), SELEC (observer), UN, UNCTAD, UNESCO, UNFICYP, UNHCR, UNIDO, UNISFA, UNMISS, UNRWA, UNSC (permanent), UPU, WCO, WHO, WIPO, WMO, WTO, ZC

Diplomatic representation in the US:

chief of mission: Ambassador Peter John WESTMACOTT

chancery: 3100 Massachusetts Avenue NW, Washington, DC 20008

telephone: [1] (202) 588-6500

FAX: [1] (202) 588-7850

consulate(s) general: Atlanta, Boston, Chicago, Denver, Houston, Los Angeles, Miami, New York, San Francisco

consulate(s): Dallas, Orlando (FL)

Diplomatic representation from the US:

chief of mission: Ambassador Louis B. SUSMAN

embassy: 24 Grosvenor Square, London, W1K 6AH note - a new embassy is scheduled to open by the end of 2017 in the Nine Elms area of Wandsworth

mailing address: PSC 801, Box 40, FPO AE 09498-4040

telephone: [44] (0) 20 7499-9000

FAX: [44] (0) 20 7629-9124

consulate(s) general: Belfast, Edinburgh

Key Leaders:

Queen	ELIZABETH II
Prime Min., First Lord of the Treasury, & Minister for the Civil Service	David William Donald CAMERON
Dep. Prime Min.	Nicholas William Peter CLEGG
Chancellor of the Exchequer	George Gideon Oliver OSBORNE
Sec. of State for Business, Innovation, & Skills	John Vincent CABLE
Sec. of State for Communities & Local Govt.	Eric PICKLES
Sec. of State for Culture, Media, & Sport	Maria MILLER
Sec. of State for	Philip HAMMOND

Defense	
Sec. of State for Education	Michael GOVE
Sec. of State for Energy & Climate Change	Edward DAVEY
Sec. of State for the Environment, Food, & Rural Affairs	Owen William PATERSON
Sec. of State for Foreign & Commonwealth Affairs	William Jefferson HAGUE
Sec. of State for Health	Jeremy HUNT
Sec. of State for the Home Dept. & Min. for Women & Equalities	Theresa Mary MAY
Sec. of State for Intl. Development	Justine GREENING
Sec. of State for Justice & Lord	Chris GRAYLING

Chancellor	
Sec. of State for Northern Ireland	Theresa Anne VILLIERS
Sec. of State for Scotland	Michael Kevin MOORE
Sec. of State for Transport	Patrick MCLOUGHLIN
Sec. of State for Wales	David JONES
Sec. of State for Work & Pensions	George Iain DUNCAN SMITH
Leader of the House of Lords & Chancellor of the Duchy of Lancaster	STRATHCLYDE, *Lord*
Leader of the House of Commons & Lord Privy Seal	Andrew LANSLEY
Min. for the Cabinet Office & Paymaster Gen.	Francis Anthony Aylmer MAUDE
Chief Sec. to the Treasury	Daniel Grian ALEXANDER

Chief Whip & Parliamentary Sec. to the Treasury	Andrew John Bower MITCHELL
Governor, Bank of England	Mervyn Allister KING
Ambassador to the US	Peter John WESTMACOTT, *Sir*
Permanent Representative to the UN, New York	Mark Justin LYALL GRANT, *Sir*

Flag description:

blue field with the red cross of Saint George (patron saint of England) edged in white superimposed on the diagonal red cross of Saint Patrick (patron saint of Ireland), which is superimposed on the diagonal white cross of Saint Andrew (patron saint of Scotland); properly known as the Union Flag, but commonly called the Union Jack; the design and colors (especially the Blue Ensign) have been the basis for a number of other flags including other Commonwealth countries and their constituent states or provinces, and British overseas territories

National symbol(s):

lion (Britain in general); lion (England); lion, unicorn (Scotland); dragon (Wales); harp (Northern Ireland)

National anthem:

name: "God Save the Queen"

lyrics/music: unknown

note: in use since 1745; by tradition, the song serves as both the national and royal anthem of the United Kingdom; it is known as either "God Save the Queen" or "God Save the King," depending on the gender of the reigning monarch; it also serves as the royal anthem of many Commonwealth nations

Chapter 5: Economy

Economy - overview:

The UK, a leading trading power and financial center, is the second largest economy in Europe after Germany. Over the past two decades, the government has greatly reduced public ownership and contained the growth of social welfare programs. Agriculture is intensive, highly mechanized, and efficient by European standards, producing about 60% of food needs with less than 2% of the labor force. The UK has large coal, natural gas, and oil resources, but its oil and natural gas reserves are declining and the UK became a net importer of energy in 2005. Services, particularly banking, insurance, and business services, account by far for the largest proportion of GDP while industry continues to decline in importance. After emerging from recession in 1992, Britain's economy enjoyed the longest period of expansion on record during which time growth outpaced most of Western Europe. In 2008, however, the global financial crisis hit the economy particularly hard, due to the importance of its financial sector. Sharply declining home prices, high consumer debt, and the global economic slowdown compounded Britain's economic problems, pushing the economy into recession in the latter half of 2008 and prompting the then BROWN (Labour) government to implement a number of measures to stimulate the economy and stabilize the financial markets; these include nationalizing parts of the banking system, temporarily cutting taxes, suspending public sector borrowing rules, and moving forward public spending on capital projects. Facing burgeoning public deficits and debt levels, in 2010 the CAMERON-led coalition government (between Conservatives and Liberal Democrats) initiated a five-year austerity program, which aimed to lower London's budget deficit from over 10% of GDP in 2010 to nearly 1% by 2015. In November 2011, Chancellor of the Exchequer George OSBORNE announced additional austerity measures through 2017 because of slower-than-expected economic growth and the impact of the euro-zone debt crisis. The CAMERON government raised the value added tax from 17.5% to 20% in 2011. It has pledged to reduce the corporation tax rate to 21% by 2014. The Bank of England (BoE) implemented an asset purchase program of up to £375 billion (approximately $605 billion) as of December 2012. During times of economic crisis, the BoE coordinates interest rate moves with the European Central Bank, but Britain remains outside the European Economic and Monetary Union (EMU). In 2012, weak consumer spending and subdued business investment weighed on the economy. GDP fell 0.1%, and the budget deficit remained stubbornly high at 7.7% of GDP. Public debt continued to increase.

GDP (purchasing power parity):
$2.323 trillion (2012 est.)
country comparison to the world: 9
$2.325 trillion (2011 est.)
$2.308 trillion (2010 est.)
note: data are in 2012 US dollars

GDP (official exchange rate):
$2.434 trillion (2012 est.)

GDP - real growth rate:
-0.1% (2012 est.)
country comparison to the world: 189
0.8% (2011 est.)
1.8% (2010 est.)

GDP - per capita (PPP):
$36,700 (2012 est.)

country comparison to the world: 36
$37,100 (2011 est.)
$37,100 (2010 est.)
note: data are in 2012 US dollars

GDP - composition by sector:
agriculture: 0.7%
industry: 21.1%
services: 78.2% (2012 est.)

Labor force:
31.9 million (2012 est.)
country comparison to the world: 20

Labor force - by occupation:
agriculture: 1.4%
industry: 18.2%
services: 80.4% (2006 est.)

Unemployment rate:
7.8% (2012 est.)
country comparison to the world: 88
8.1% (2011 est.)

Population below poverty line:
14% (2006 est.)

Household income or consumption by percentage share:
lowest 10%: 2.1%
highest 10%: 28.5% (1999)

Distribution of family income - Gini index:
40 (FY08/09)
country comparison to the world: 60
34 (2005)

Investment (gross fixed):
13.9% of GDP (2012 est.)
country comparison to the world: 140

Budget:
revenues: $995.9 billion
expenditures: $1.183 trillion (2012 est.)

Taxes and other revenues:
40.9% of GDP (2012 est.)
country comparison to the world: 44

Budget surplus (+) or deficit (-):
-7.7% of GDP (2012 est.)
country comparison to the world: 194

Public debt:
88.7% of GDP (2012 est.)
country comparison to the world: 19
85% of GDP (2011 est.)
note: data cover general government debt, and include debt instruments issued (or owned) by government entities other than the treasury; the data include treasury debt held by foreign entities; the data include

debt issued by subnational entities, as well as intra-governmental debt; intra-governmental debt consists of treasury borrowings from surpluses in the social funds, such as for retirement, medical care, and unemployment; debt instruments for the social funds are not sold at public auctions

Inflation rate (consumer prices):

2.8% (2012 est.)

country comparison to the world: 64

4.5% (2011 est.)

Central bank discount rate:

0.5% (31 December 2012 est.)

country comparison to the world: 140

0.5% (31 December 2011 est.)

Commercial bank prime lending rate:

4% (31 December 2012 est.)

country comparison to the world: 168

4.06% (31 December 2011 est.)

Stock of narrow money:

$100.9 billion (31 December 2012 est.)

country comparison to the world: 35

$92.77 billion (31 December 2011 est.)

Stock of broad money:

$3.884 trillion (31 December 2011 est.)

country comparison to the world: 6
$4.116 trillion (31 December 2010 est.)

Stock of domestic credit:
$3.578 trillion (31 December 2012 est.)
country comparison to the world: 6
$3.671 trillion (31 December 2011 est.)

Market value of publicly traded shares:
$1.202 trillion (31 December 2011)
country comparison to the world: 5
$3.107 trillion (31 December 2010)
$2.796 trillion (31 December 2009)

Agriculture - products:
cereals, oilseed, potatoes, vegetables; cattle, sheep, poultry; fish

Industries:
machine tools, electric power equipment, automation equipment, railroad equipment, shipbuilding, aircraft, motor vehicles and parts, electronics and communications equipment, metals, chemicals, coal, petroleum, paper and paper products, food processing, textiles, clothing, other consumer goods

Industrial production growth rate:
-1.2% (2011 est.)
country comparison to the world: 154

Current account balance:
    -$57.7 billion (2012 est.)
    country comparison to the world: 187
    -$46.04 billion (2011 est.)

Exports:
    $481 billion (2012 est.)
    country comparison to the world: 12
    $479.2 billion (2011 est.)

Exports - commodities:
    manufactured goods, fuels, chemicals; food, beverages, tobacco

Exports - partners:
    Germany 10.9%, US 9.9%, Netherlands 7.9%, France 7.4%, Switzerland 7.1%, Ireland 6%, Belgium 5.3% (2011)

Imports:
    $646 billion (2012 est.)
    country comparison to the world: 7
    $639 billion (2011 est.)

Imports - commodities:
    manufactured goods, machinery, fuels; foodstuffs

Imports - partners:

Germany 12.5%, China 8.2%, Netherlands 7.1%, US 7%, France 5.7%, Belgium 4.8%, Norway 4.7% (2011)

Reserves of foreign exchange and gold:
$94.54 billion (31 December 2011 est.)
country comparison to the world: 24
$82.41 billion (2010 est.)

Debt - external:
$9.836 trillion (30 June 2011)
country comparison to the world: 3
$8.981 trillion (30 June 2010)

Stock of direct foreign investment - at home:
$1.262 trillion (31 December 2012 est.)
country comparison to the world: 3
$1.201 trillion (31 December 2011 est.)

Stock of direct foreign investment - abroad:
$1.793 trillion (31 December 2012 est.)
country comparison to the world: 2
$1.705 trillion (31 December 2011 est.)

Exchange rates:
British pounds (GBP) per US dollar -
0.6324 (2012 est.)
0.624 (2011 est.)
0.6472 (2010 est.)

0.6175 (2009)

0.5302 (2008)

Fiscal year:

6 April - 5 April

Chapter 6: Energy

Electricity - production:
    352.7 billion kWh (2010 est.)
    country comparison to the world: 13

Electricity - consumption:
    325.8 billion kWh (2009 est.)
    country comparison to the world: 13

Electricity - exports:
    4.481 billion kWh (2010 est.)
    country comparison to the world: 30

Electricity - imports:
    7.144 billion kWh (2010 est.)
    country comparison to the world: 32

Electricity - installed generating capacity:
    88.02 million kW (2009 est.)
    country comparison to the world: 13

Electricity - from fossil fuels:
    75.4% of total installed capacity (2009 est.)
    country comparison to the world: 98

Electricity - from nuclear fuels:
    12.3% of total installed capacity (2009 est.)
    country comparison to the world: 17

Electricity - from hydroelectric plants:

1.9% of total installed capacity (2009 est.)

country comparison to the world: 137

Electricity - from other renewable sources:

7.3% of total installed capacity (2009 est.)

country comparison to the world: 27

Crude oil - production:

1.099 million bbl/day (2011 est.)

country comparison to the world: 20

Crude oil - exports:

788,900 bbl/day (2009 est.)

country comparison to the world: 17

Crude oil - imports:

942,100 bbl/day (2009 est.)

country comparison to the world: 12

Crude oil - proved reserves:

2.827 billion bbl (1 January 2013 est.)

country comparison to the world: 32

Refined petroleum products - production:

1.584 million bbl/day (2009 est.)

country comparison to the world: 16

Refined petroleum products - consumption:

1.608 million bbl/day (2011 est.)

country comparison to the world: 16

Refined petroleum products - exports:

535,300 bbl/day (2009 est.)

country comparison to the world: 14

Refined petroleum products - imports:

493,500 bbl/day (2009 est.)

country comparison to the world: 13

Natural gas - production:

47.43 billion cu m (2011 est.)

country comparison to the world: 21

Natural gas - consumption:

82.21 billion cu m (2011 est.)

country comparison to the world: 10

Natural gas - exports:

16.69 billion cu m (2011 est.)

country comparison to the world: 18

Natural gas - imports:

53.43 billion cu m (2011 est.)

country comparison to the world: 7

Natural gas - proved reserves:

253 billion cu m (1 January 2012 est.)

country comparison to the world: 44

Carbon dioxide emissions from consumption of energy:

532.4 million Mt (2010 est.)

country comparison to the world: 11

Chapter 7: Communications

Telephones - main lines in use:
    33.23 million (2011)
    country comparison to the world: 9

Telephones - mobile cellular:
    81.612 million (2012)
    country comparison to the world: 17

Telephone system:
    general assessment: technologically advanced domestic and international system
    domestic: equal mix of buried cables, microwave radio relay, and fiber-optic systems
    international: country code - 44; numerous submarine cables provide links throughout Europe, Asia, Australia, the Middle East, and US; satellite earth stations - 10 Intelsat (7 Atlantic Ocean and 3 Indian Ocean), 1 Inmarsat (Atlantic Ocean region), and 1 Eutelsat; at least 8 large international switching centers (2011)

Broadcast media:
    public service broadcaster, British Broadcasting Corporation (BBC), is the largest broadcasting corporation in the world; BBC operates multiple TV

networks with regional and local TV service; a mixed system of public and commercial TV broadcasters along with satellite and cable systems provide access to hundreds of TV stations throughout the world; BBC operates multiple national, regional, and local radio networks with multiple transmission sites; a large number of commercial radio stations as well as satellite radio services are available (2008)

Internet country code:

.uk

Internet hosts:

8.107 million (2012)

country comparison to the world: 15

Internet users:

51.444 million (2009)

country comparison to the world: 7

Chapter 8: Transportation

Airports:
    462 (2012)
    country comparison to the world: 19

Airports - with paved runways:
    total: 272
    over 3,047 m: 7
    2,438 to 3,047 m: 31
    1,524 to 2,437 m: 93
    914 to 1,523 m: 76
    under 914 m: 65 (2012)

Airports - with unpaved runways:
    total: 190
    1,524 to 2,437 m: 2
    914 to 1,523 m: 25
    under 914 m: 163 (2012)

Heliports:
    9 (2012)

Pipelines:
    condensate 8 km; gas 14,071 km; liquid petroleum gas 59 km; oil 595 km; refined products 4,907 km (2010)

Railways:

total: 16,454 km

country comparison to the world: 17

broad gauge: 303 km 1.600-m gauge (in Northern Ireland)

standard gauge: 16,151 km 1.435-m gauge (5,248 km electrified) (2008)

Roadways:

total: 394,428 km

country comparison to the world: 16

paved: 394,428 km (includes 3,519 km of expressways) (2009)

Waterways:

3,200 km (620 km used for commerce) (2009)

country comparison to the world: 32

Merchant marine:

total: 504

country comparison to the world: 22

by type: bulk carrier 33, cargo 76, carrier 4, chemical tanker 58, container 178, liquefied gas 6, passenger 7, passenger/cargo 66, petroleum tanker 18, refrigerated cargo 2, roll on/roll off 31, vehicle carrier 25

foreign-owned: 271 (Australia 1, Bermuda 6, China 7, Denmark 43, France 39, Germany 59, Hong Kong 12,

Ireland 1, Italy 3, Japan 5, Netherlands 1, Norway 32, Sweden 28, Taiwan 11, Tanzania 1, UAE 8, US 14) registered in other countries: 308 (Algeria 15, Antigua and Barbuda 1, Argentina 2, Australia 5, Bahamas 18, Barbados 6, Belgium 2, Belize 4, Bermuda 14, Bolivia 1, Brunei 2, Cambodia 1, Cape Verde 1, Cayman Islands 2, Comoros 1, Cook Islands 2, Cyprus 7, Georgia 5, Gibraltar 6, Greece 6, Honduras 1, Hong Kong 33, Indonesia 2, Italy 2, Liberia 22, Liberia 32, Luxembourg 5, Malta 21, Marshall Islands 12, Marshall Islands 3, Moldova 3, Nigeria 2, NZ 1, Panama 37, Panama 5, Saint Kitts and Nevis 1, Saint Vincent and the Grenadines 6, Sierra Leone 1, Singapore 6, Thailand 6, Tonga 1, US 4, unknown 1) (2010)

Ports and terminals:

Dover, Felixstowe, Immingham, Liverpool, London, Southampton, Teesport (England); Forth Ports (Scotland); Milford Haven (Wales)

oil terminals: Fawley Marine terminal, Liverpool Bay terminal (England); Braefoot Bay terminal, Finnart oil terminal, Hound Point terminal (Scotland)

Chapter 9: Military

Military branches:
Army, Royal Navy (includes Royal Marines), Royal Air Force (2010)

Military service age and obligation:
16-33 years of age (officers 17-28) for voluntary military service (with parental consent under 18); women serve in military services, but are excluded from ground combat positions and some naval postings; as of October 2009, women comprised 12.1% of officers and 9% of enlisted personnel in the regular forces; must be citizen of the UK, Commonwealth, or Republic of Ireland; reservists serve a minimum of 3 years, to age 45 or 55; 16 years of age for voluntary military service by Nepalese citizens in the Brigade of Gurkhas; 16-34 years of age for voluntary military service by Papua New Guinean citizens (2009)

Manpower available for military service:
males age 16-49: 14,856,917
females age 16-49: 14,307,316 (2010 est.)

Manpower fit for military service:
males age 16-49: 12,255,452

females age 16-49: 11,779,679 (2010 est.)

Manpower reaching militarily significant age annually:

male: 383,989

female: 365,491 (2010 est.)

Military expenditures:

2.5% of GDP (2012)

country comparison to the world: 56

Chapter 10: Transnational Issues

Disputes - international:
in 2002, Gibraltar residents voted overwhelmingly by referendum to reject any "shared sovereignty" arrangement between the UK and Spain; the Government of Gibraltar insisted on equal participation in talks between the two countries; Spain disapproved of UK plans to grant Gibraltar greater autonomy; Mauritius and Seychelles claim the Chagos Archipelago (British Indian Ocean Territory); in 2001, the former inhabitants of the archipelago, evicted 1967 - 1973, were granted U.K. citizenship and the right of return, followed by Orders in Council in 2004 that banned rehabitation, a High Court ruling reversed the ban, a Court of Appeal refusal to hear the case, and a Law Lords' decision in 2008 denied the right of return; in addition, the United Kingdom created the world's largest marine protection area around the Chagos islands prohibiting the extraction of any natural resources therein; UK rejects sovereignty talks requested by Argentina, which still claims the Falkland Islands (Islas Malvinas) and South Georgia and the South Sandwich Islands;

territorial claim in Antarctica (British Antarctic Territory) overlaps Argentine claim and partially overlaps Chilean claim; Iceland, the UK, and Ireland dispute Denmark's claim that the Faroe Islands' continental shelf extends beyond 200 nm

Refugees and internally displaced persons:
refugees (country of origin): 19,668 Somalia; 15,652 Iraq; 14,424 Afghanistan; 11,632 Iran; 9,851 Eritrea; 5,776 Turkey; 5,737 Sri Lanka (2011)

Illicit drugs:
producer of limited amounts of synthetic drugs and synthetic precursor chemicals; major consumer of Southwest Asian heroin, Latin American cocaine, and synthetic drugs; money-laundering center

Map of the United Kingdom

Other Key Facts™ Titles

Key Facts on Syria

Key Facts on China

Key Facts on Qatar

Key Facts on India

Key Facts on Germany

Key Facts on Argentina

Key Facts on Russia

Key Facts on North Korea

Key Facts on Brazil

Key Facts on Italy

Key Facts on the United Arab Emirates

Key Facts on the European Union

Key Facts on Pakistan

Key Facts on Saudi Arabia

Key Facts on Cyprus

Key Facts on Iran

Key Facts on Afghanistan

Key Facts on Iraq

Key Facts on Indonesia

Key Facts on South Korea

Key Facts on France

All Key Facts™ Titles are Available at www.Amazon.com

THE INTERNATIONALIST®
2013
WWW.INTERNATIONALIST.COM

www.ingramcontent.com/pod-product-compliance
Lightning Source LLC
Chambersburg PA
CBHW071642170526
45166CB00003B/1402